Willie Mays

YOUNG SUPERSTAR

Willie Mays
YOUNG SUPERSTAR

by Louis Sabin
illustrated by John R. Jones

Troll Associates

Library of Congress Cataloging-in-Publication Data

Sabin, Louis.
    Willie Mays, young superstar / by Louis Sabin; illustrated by
John R. Jones.
        p.   cm.
    Summary: A brief biography, emphasizing the early life, of the
record-setting baseball player who is one of three in the game's
history to hit 600 home runs.
    ISBN 0-8167-1775-3 (lib. bdg.)   ISBN 0-8167-1776-1 (pbk.)
    1. Mays, Willie, 1931-   —Juvenile literature.   2. Baseball players—
United States—Biography—Juvenile literature.   [1. Mays, Willie,
1931-   —Childhood and youth.   2. Baseball players.   3. Afro-
Americans—Biography.]   I. Jones, John R., ill.   II. Title.
GV865.M38S25   1990
796.357 '092—dc20
    [B]   89-33979

Willie Mays

YOUNG SUPERSTAR

Baseball history is filled with the names of great athletes and champions. But nobody ever played the game with more joy, style, and natural ability than Willie Mays. He was a fan's dream come true.

Willie Mays could do it all. He hit—and hit with power. He ran with the speed and grace of a greyhound. He threw with strength and accuracy. And he chased down and caught hit balls that other fielders might have given up on. Willie was a "natural," an athlete with amazing ability. Many people think he was the greatest ball player who ever lived.

Willie was born on May 6, 1931, in Westfield, Alabama. Both of his parents were eighteen years old and just out of high school. Willie's mother, Ann, was a high-school track star. She set a number of records as a runner in Westfield. His father, William Howard Mays, was a fine outfielder in Birmingham, Alabama's Industrial League. Sports played a big part in Willie's life from his very first days.

At the time Willie was born, his father was working in a steel mill. The job he had was low paying. Mr. Mays knew he would never make much money working in the steel mill. The doors of opportunity were often shut for black people

in those days. Still, he wanted his son to have
a better life than he had. And playing sports for
a living seemed to be the best answer.

Mr. Mays had dreamed of being a star baseball
player himself. But marriage and fatherhood
made that almost impossible. So he dreamed the
good life for his son.

Willie Mays was an active baby. He took his first steps when he was just six months old. Right away, his father introduced him to sports. "As soon as he started walking," Willie's father recalled, "I bought him a big round ball. He'd hold that ball and then he'd bounce it and chase it. And if he ever couldn't get that ball, he'd cry."

Willie Mays and a ball—it was a perfect combination. Mr. Mays put a baseball on one chair. He put another chair a couple of feet away. Then he stood little Willie by the second chair. "See the ball?" his father asked. "Can you get it?" The baby smiled and toddled to the ball. He grabbed it in both hands, laughing happily. "Great!" Mr. Mays cried. "Now, give Daddy the ball."

They played this game over and over. Each time, Mr. Mays moved the chairs a little farther apart. Soon, baby Willie was toddling across the entire room to get the ball. That was Willie Mays' first fielding lesson in baseball.

Batting lessons came next. Mr. Mays sat Willie in the middle of the floor. He gave the baby a stick about two feet long. Then the father sat down and rolled the ball to his son. "Can you hit the ball?" Mr. Mays asked. "Come on, hit the ball to Daddy."

Little Willie giggled. This game was fun. A ball and a stick were his favorite toys. He spent hours playing with the ball. He hit it with the stick. Then he chased it across the room and hit it again with the stick. Willie never grew tired of this simple game. Even when he went to sleep, he kept the ball and stick next to him.

13

When Willie Mays was three years old, his parents were divorced. Willie stayed with his father. Mr. Mays adored his bright-eyed little boy and wanted Willie with him. But that left Mr. Mays with a problem.

For a year, Mr. Mays had been working at a different job, with the railroad. He took care of passengers' luggage on a train that went back and forth between Birmingham, Alabama, and Detroit, Michigan. This job paid more than the job he had at the mill. Mr. Mays hoped to save enough money to buy something special—his own home in a nice neighborhood. He wanted his son to grow up in a warm, comfortable house. So he saved every nickel he could for that house he wanted so much.

But the problem Mr. Mays had was that his railroad job often kept him away from home. He needed someone to look after his little boy. Then a neighbor died, and her two daughters needed a home. Mr. Mays took them in.

The teen-age girls were named Sarah and Ernestine. All at once, Willie had a family. Sarah and Ernestine were like mothers and sisters and good friends to the three-year-old boy. When Daddy was away, they made sure Willie was clean and fed and safe. This was a wonderful help to Mr. Mays.

It was a wonderful arrangement for the girls, too. The kindness of Mr. Mays kept them from being homeless. So they were just as happy to be a part of Mr. Mays' family as he was to have them. And Willie loved the girls. He called them Aunt Sarah and Aunt Ernestine. That was his way of showing them love and respect.

16

When he was away on train trips, Mr. Mays missed Willie very much. He wanted to be home with his son more than he was. So even though the steel mill job paid less money, Mr. Mays went back to work there. He was glad to be with his little boy again. However, he was also a little sad. Now he had to put off the dream of owning his own home.

The Westfield house Mr. Mays lived in was owned by the steel company. Mr. Mays paid rent. In fact, the steel company owned most of the land and businesses in Westfield, Alabama. Workers at the mill were not paid in money. Instead, they were paid in company chips each Friday.

When a mill worker needed new clothing, he bought it at one of the company stores in the mill. When a mill worker needed food, he bought it at another company store. The bills were paid with chips.

The steel company had great control over its workers. The company paid only in chips. And only company stores accepted chips as payment. So the workers had to buy everything from the company.

The money Mr. Mays had earned while working for the railroad was put into a bank account. He added to it by doing part-time work that paid real money, not chips. He also played baseball for a semiprofessional team. The pay wasn't much, but every penny of it went into Mr. Mays' "dream house" bank account. Ernestine also contributed to the family income. She worked as a waitress in a local restaurant.

Ernestine gave Willie money each week so he could buy lunch at school. There was no school cafeteria. Every day, Willie and his friends went to a nearby grocery store. Willie bought bread, lunch meat, fruit, cake, and milk. Then the children went to an empty lot and shared the food. In the evening, Willie often brought friends home for dinner. Sarah would then feed them all.

Willie Mays didn't know that his family was poor. The house was comfortable. There was enough food to eat. And Willie was always told to share his lunch money and to invite friends home for dinner. As poor as Willie's family was, his friends' families were even poorer.

Willie was growing up in the 1930s, the time of the Great Depression. Millions of Americans were out of work. There was hunger and homelessness in every part of the country. So Willie was lucky. His father and Ernestine had jobs. And Sarah was a good homemaker. She saw to it that every dollar went a long way.

Willie was surrounded by kindness and love. Without ever making a big thing of it, the Mays family gave true meaning to the word "charity." Willie came to understand this when he was a grown man.

Even as a child, Willie's world was centered around baseball. And he was good, right from the start. He rushed out of school every day, ready to play. The vacant lot where Willie and his friends ate lunch became a ball field in the afternoon.

Willie and his friends played with the barest of equipment. They had no uniforms. They had no special shoes or spikes, no catcher's mask or chest protector, and no batting helmet. Most of the children didn't even own a glove. They used a stick as a bat and played with whatever ball was available. They just chose up sides and played for the fun of it.

When it was time to choose sides, Willie was one of the first picked. Sometimes, older children played on the lot. Even then, Willie was welcome as a player. He could run, throw, slide, hit, and catch the ball as well as any boy in town.

Willie's eyesight was better than normal. He could look straight ahead and see things that were happening in front and on both sides of him. Many great athletes have this wide range of vision. It helps them to see everything going on in the game. This is true in baseball, basketball, football, and many other sports.

Willie also had very large hands. "I knew he'd be a good ball player," Mr. Mays remembered. "It's those big hands of his. With hands that big, he never had trouble catching the ball."

Willie did have big hands for his age. He also had great timing and speed. And most of all, he worked at learning to catch well. Whenever Mr. Mays had a moment to spare, he played ball with his son. They started when Willie was five years old. Father and son had a special game. Mr. Mays bounced the ball to Willie. The boy caught it after one bounce and threw it back. They did this for hours at a time. It was like the game they played when Willie was just learning to walk.

Mr. Mays did something even more special. When he went to play in Industrial League games, he took Willie with him. The little boy was allowed to sit on the bench with the grown-up players. It was a thrill for Willie. It was fun for Mr. Mays, too. And there was another advantage to having Willie in the dugout. The whole team acted as baby sitters while Mr. Mays was playing.

Willie got much more than fun out of those days. He listened to everything the players said. They talked about batting against different kinds of pitchers. They talked about stealing bases. They chatted about how to play on wet or very rough fields. They talked about bunting, and how to catch a ball cleanly and then throw it quickly to the right base. Everything it took to play the game well was mentioned in that dugout. Willie listened because it was so interesting. He didn't realize that he was getting a priceless education in the sport.

Before the games, the players stayed in the locker room. Then Willie was free to run all over the field. He made believe he was his father stealing second base . . . third base . . . home. He slid hard into each bag. He loved running and sliding into one base after another. After all this sliding, Willie's clothes were very dirty. Sarah complained about how dirty Willie got while his father was playing. It was a joke she liked to repeat after every game.

Willie copied the moves his father made on the field. Mr. Mays was an excellent outfielder. He could run down balls hit anywhere in his part of the outfield. He made amazing catches and equally amazing throws. This ability to pounce on a hit ball with speed and smoothness earned Mr. Mays the nicknames "Kitty-Kat" and "Cat."

Willie worked hard to be just like his father. This made Mr. Mays very happy. He hoped that his son would be a professional baseball player. But he did not push Willie. Baseball had to be something Willie wanted. And Willie certainly wanted to play the game. His love of baseball grew even stronger when he learned that his father was paid to play. "That seemed to me," Willie Mays remembered, "just about the nicest idea anyone ever thought up."

To Willie Mays, both as a child and as an adult, the sport was pure joy. The fans could feel Willie's delight. It was in the way he ran, taking swift, sure strides. It was in the way he raced around the bases. It was in dozens of unforgettable catches and throws. It was in the ball-crushing swing of his bat. It was in his wide grin and the way his hat flew off as he ran to catch a ball or take an extra base. And it was in the way he said "Say hey!" to express his pleasure at one thing or another. Willie Mays simply loved the game!

Young Willie also enjoyed other sports. Like many boys, he played whatever sport was in season. In the fall, it was football. In the winter, it was both football and basketball. But best of all was baseball, which he played in the spring, summer, and fall.

When Willie was ten years old, the family finally moved into the "dream house" Mr. Mays always wanted. It was a neat cottage in a Birmingham suburb called Fairfield. There was a grassy lawn, a big front porch, and a nice back yard. It wasn't a large house, but Mr. Mays owned it. At last, he didn't have to pay rent for a company house.

Willie liked his new neighborhood and his new school. Soon, he made friends with a boy who lived a few houses away. The boy's name was

Charlie Willis. Willie and Charlie became best friends, and they stayed best friends from then on.

The boys were both crazy about sports, movies, and comic books. They walked to school together, throwing a ball back and forth. They shared comic books, went to the movies together regularly, and listened to the radio together. If Charlie and Willie weren't playing ball outside, they were in each other's house. The boys were as close as brothers.

Willie called Charlie "Cool," and Charlie called Willie "Buck." These nicknames stuck with them even as grown-ups. But Willie the professional ball player was never called Buck by his teammates. It was a name used only by people who knew him as a boy in Birmingham, Alabama.

33

When Willie was about twelve years old, he fell
out of a tree and broke his right arm. At first,
Willie didn't know his arm was broken. He rushed
home, paying no attention to the pain. He was
more upset about falling and looking silly. He was
also worried about being punished for climbing
a tree. That was something his father had told
him not to do. When the pain got worse, Willie
could no longer hide it. He told his father everything. Mr. Mays didn't punish Willie. He just
made sure the doctor took care of his arm.

When Willie's arm was healed, it was very
strong. Before the break, he threw underhand.
Those throws were good but not great. After
the arm healed, Willie was more comfortable
throwing overhand. And his throws were faster,
stronger, and more accurate than ever.

One day, while Willie was playing baseball with
his friends, he was asked to play with the Gray
Sox. It was a semiprofessional team in Fairfield.
All the other players were at least two years
older than the thirteen-year-old Mays boy. Willie
was quick to say yes.

At first, Willie played shortstop. That didn't
last long. His excitement got the better of him.
Every time he fielded the ball, he threw it to
first base as hard as he could. It was so hard
that the first baseman complained.

"Willie," the manager said, "I think your arm's
too good to waste at shortstop. I want you to pitch
our next game."

Willie was thrilled at the idea. He knew every-body watched the pitcher. The pitcher was the star—the game was in his hands. And Willie became an instant star. The crowd cheered him as he pitched the Gray Sox's next game. His fast ball was too much for the other team to hit.

After the game, Willie couldn't wait to get home. He wanted to tell his father about his fantastic pitching. Mr. Mays listened silently. When Willie was finished, his father praised him. Then Mr. Mays asked Willie not to pitch another game. Willie didn't understand until his father explained why.

"If a pitcher hurts his arm," Mr. Mays said, "he's finished in baseball . . . unless he knows how to play the *whole* game. Now, most pitchers never bother to learn anything but pitching. I don't want that to happen to you. You've got to work on hitting, fielding, throwing—everything. Maybe you will be a pitcher someday, maybe not. But whatever you are, you'll be a complete ball player. I don't want you to waste your whole future by trying to be a star at thirteen."

Willie was disappointed, but he obeyed his father. He knew Mr. Mays was really wise when it came to baseball. The boy worked on improving his all-around game and left pitching to other players on the team. His father proved to be right, and Willie had a long career. He reached the Major Leagues in 1951 and played for twenty-three years.

During the summers of 1945 and 1946, Willie played in the Industrial League with his father. Mr. Mays was in center field, and Willie was in left field. The teen-ager was getting better every game. The father was getting a little slower every game. Near the end of the 1946 season, something happened that Willie never forgot. A ball was hit into left-center field. Mr. Mays called out, "I'll take it!" Willie saw that his father would not get to the ball in time. So Willie cut in front of his father and gloved the ball just before it hit the ground.

Willie and his father never talked about that moment. But Mr. Mays stopped playing baseball after the 1946 summer season ended. He felt sad for himself but very proud of his son. He showed his pride by taking Willie to meet Piper Davis, manager of the Birmingham Black Barons. They were one of the top teams in the Negro Leagues. Mr. Mays wanted Davis to give Willie a tryout for the Black Barons.

At the time, the Negro Leagues were the only place in the U.S. where black athletes could play pro baseball. They were not allowed in the Major Leagues. The black teams were just as good as those in the Major Leagues. That became clear in 1947. It was the year former Negro League star Jackie Robinson became the first black player in the Major Leagues. As a member of the Brooklyn Dodgers, Jackie was an instant Major League star. He was soon followed by other fine players from the Negro Leagues. Among them were Hank Aaron, Roy Campanella, Larry Doby, Monte Irvin, and Satchel Paige.

When Willie Mays was growing up, his dream was to play for the Black Barons. Because of segregation, he never imagined himself playing in the Major Leagues. So he was thrilled to be given a tryout by Piper Davis.

Willie did well at his tryout and was invited to join the Black Barons. That's when Mr. Mays set down the rules. Willie had to get good grades and finish high school. He was allowed to play on weekends and during summer vacations. But if Willie's grades slipped, it meant no baseball. Even if Willie didn't like the rules, he had to accept them. He was too young to sign a contract for himself. Besides, Willie knew that his father had his best interests at heart.

There was someone else looking after Willie's best interests. He was E.T. Oliver, the principal of Fairfield Industrial High School. Mr. Oliver kept a close eye on Willie. He made sure Willie gave full attention to his schoolwork. Mr. Oliver really cared about his students. He had strict but fair rules. "Get educated," he told the students.

And they knew he meant it. Mr. Oliver felt that good grades and good behavior came *before* sports and social life.

Willie Mays always remembered Mr. Oliver with respect. Willie was proud and pleased to say he was a high-school graduate. Many Major Leaguers today go to college. But when Willie was playing, many ball players did not finish high school. That might not have hurt them while they were playing ball. But it did once they were finished, because they did not have the skills and education for a new career.

With high school behind him, Willie became a full-time player with the Black Barons. And now that the Major Leagues were open to black ball players, the scouts were keeping a close watch on Willie. They saw him hit over .300 for the 1948 and 1949 seasons. His hitting and fielding made him a first-rate prospect. Then, in the middle of the 1950 season, Willie Mays was signed by the New York Giants of the National League. They gave him a small amount of money for signing. After that, they sent him to New Jersey to play for the Trenton Giants. It was a Class B minor league team.

Willie remembered that time clearly. "I realized I was a pioneer," he said. "Not only was I the first black player on the Trenton Giants, I was the first in the entire league."

Mays was sensational with Trenton. The next year, he was moved up to the Minneapolis Millers. The Millers were a Triple-A team in the American Association. That meant the nineteen-year-old superstar was one step from the Major Leagues.

After thirty-five games at Minneapolis, Willie was batting a league-leading .477! At that point, he was brought up to the New York Giants. Willie Mays was a Major Leaguer at last!

Willie was scared, however, and didn't get a hit in the first few games he played. He was ashamed and ready to quit. But Manager Leo Durocher wouldn't let him. "As long as I'm manager of the Giants," Durocher told him, "you're my center fielder. You're here to stay. Stop worrying. With your talent, you're going to get plenty of hits."

Mays did just that. He helped the Giants win the 1951 National League pennant in an exciting race with the Brooklyn Dodgers. He won Rookie of the Year honors that year. But perhaps most important of all, he won the hearts of baseball fans everywhere. It was a love affair that lasted his entire career.

Willie started his Major League career with the Giants in New York. When the team moved to San Francisco, he continued to be a Giant star. Then, to the joy of New Yorkers, he joined the New York Mets in 1972. Willie played two seasons with the Mets, helping them win the National League pennant in 1973. After that, he retired.

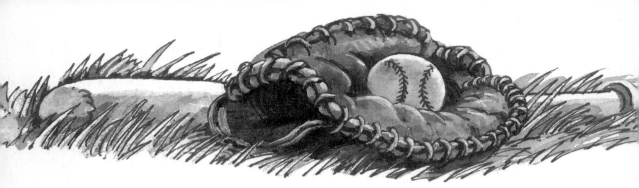

During his career, Willie Mays slugged 660 home runs. Only Hank Aaron and Babe Ruth ever hit more. Twice, Willie hit 50 or more homers in a single season. In 1954, he showed what a complete hitter he was by winning the National League batting title. At one time or another, he also led the National League in triples, runs, hits, stolen bases, and bases on balls. And he played great defense in the outfield. It came as no surprise to anyone when Willie was elected to the Baseball Hall of Fame in 1979. It was the first year he was eligible, and he was voted in on the first ballot.

For millions of fans, Willie Mays *was* baseball. He was a brilliant hitter, base runner, and fielder. And his bubbly personality won him friends and admirers everywhere. No player ever gave more to the game than Willie Mays. He was truly a fan's dream come true.

Date Due			

cop.1

E
B
MAY

Sabin, Louis
    Willie Mays,
      young superstar

Grades 4-6   92